FOREIGN TALES OF EXEMPLUM AND WOE

FOREIGN TALES OF EXEMPLUM AND WOE

J.C. ELLEFSON

Fomite
Burlington, Vt

ISBN-13: 978-1-937677-82-4
Library of Congress Control Number: 2015936443

Cover image:
Cañadón del Río Pinturas, Cueva de las manos, Santa Cruz, Argentina
Copyright © Pablo Gimenez 2012
Made available under a Creative Commons Attribution-Share Alike 2.0 license (https://creativecommons.org/licenses/by-sa/2.0/)

Fomite
58 Peru Street
Burlington, VT 05401
www.fomitepress.com

ACKNOWLEDGEMENTS

Antigonish Review: "Denying The Afternoon..."
Ariel: "Belated Letter Of Thanks"
Berkeley Poetry Review: "The Inscrutable Miss Me Li..."; "Little Anna Of God"
Chaminade: "For The T'ai Chi Master..."; "The Return Of The Inscrutable Miss Mei Li"
Clutch: "Down At The Shanghai Soul Exchange"
College English: "Sadie's Last Love Letter"
Fine Madness: "Checking In On Dash"
Green Mountains Review: "Dream Of Returning..."; "Miss Zhou's Essay..."; "Willie Li..."
Hambone: "A Foreign Tale..."; "Around Midnight..."
Hampden–Sydney Poetry Review: "Expatriate Babble"; "We Gypsies"
International Poetry Review: "Somewhere In The Middle. . ."; "Denying The Afternoon. . ."
Jeopardy: "A Cerebral Return..."
Lullwater: "In The Middle Of The Tall Night"
Malahat: "Circling The House And Grounds..."; "Postcard From The Cobbleston City"
Mudfish: "Re-Composing Ms. Tan Dan"; "Love Letter..."
New Orleans Review: "Inheriting The Crazy Man's Desk"
Orbis: "Letter Of Thanks..."; "The House Called Nossa Senhora..."
Permafrost: "...Mr. Fu Escapes..."; "...Nature Boy"
Plaza: "How To Arrive In Far Away Places"
Puerto Del Sol: "On The Bus"
Virginia Quarterly: "The Available Supporting Roles..."

West Branch: "The Expatriate Returns To Dream Street"
Wisconsin Review: "Another Tune Played Blue"; "Everyday Somewhere Along The Big Road"
Xenophilia: "Love And Death Girl"

"A fisherman names his boat after his mother and his wife."
— Alan Dugan

This book is for JoAnn Wright, Nancy Means Wright, and Lesley Ashworth Wright.

There's no use trying to explain it. Let us now praise unconditional love.

"But oh! shipmates! on the starboard hand of every woe, there is a sure delight…"

Father Mapple, *Moby Dick*

CONTENTS

MOTHER ROAD'S TRAVELERS' ADVISORY FOR CROSSING THE LANDS OF THE INFIDELS

First, you must never tell them the truth. Never
tell them where you've been, or where
you're going — and never show them
who you are. It's far better to find out
who they are and tell them
you're the same. Tell them
you went to the same school, played
the same sports, drive the same
car. You can even say their words, but if you
say their words long enough you'll
believe them. You might even come to believe
their words to be your own, but this
you'll find to be a painful and dangerous
situation. You see, this is when
you'll crumble into your own pathetic
dust, writhe in your own slime. So for
safety's sake, if there must be talk, I suggest
you do it allegorically. I suggest you let them

circle at your knees in the suspense of some
titillating provocative tale. Let them
circle around you and tell them
when you were young and mouthy you gave
your life away. You tell them this. Tell them
you sat across a wide smooth table from a little
round man with a ham-fat face and traded
everything you were going to get — the pretty
blonde wife and daughter, the cute little

bread and butter house at the end of the tree-
lined street, your shined shoes and parking
space at the club — even the sweet ambrosial
laughter that would greet you when you'd
stiffly walk into a warm holiday room
filled with realistic nineteenth century
landscapes and creamy soft food. And for
all of it, you tell them you got the keys
to the highway, and a terminal case of the goes.

Now, pause a moment and let them chew on your
words, but remember, if they chew on your words
long enough, they'll take them for their own —
and I promise you they'll soon chew your bones — so in
lieu of a painful and dangerous experience, I suggest
you distract them a bit. Reach deep into your left hand
pants pocket and pull out the keys — like they're
so many jewels. You just pull out
the keys and pass them around on the palm
of your hand to their accompaniment of little
soft grunts and squeals, well elocuted shrill
oinks. And you do this with a smile
on your face — because there's never
any reason not to be nice — but for safety's
sake: don't linger, shake hands, wave, bow, keep
your back to the wall, and be nice on your way
to the door, telling them it's been a fun
party — and how much you've enjoyed yourself —
but somehow, good God, it's gotten so
late, and you can hear your mother calling.

Down At The Shanghai Soul Exchange

Welcome to the crowded city. Welcome
to crowded hopes. Welcome to Loud Town — a million
faces in the windows — a million faces
disappear into the city built on mud
and despair — where the chiseled woman who serves
noodles could have danced Swan Lake, and the sweet
wall-eyed man who feeds roses
buckets of shit hums a dispassionate
Mozart between the flower beds. The whiskey
faced professor keeps his stiff mouth shut
inside his suit jacket, and the young girl
whose father was beaten to death by the Red
Guard wants to serve you steamy
vegetables at the end of every
antithetical day because this silly girl
loves you. This silly girl wants your heart — the big
light, big faced human plane ticket for every
hungry ghost and thirsty spirit — the compassionate
personification of the land
of the free and the home of the brave.
Everyone's favorite altruist. You can
see it in the million blank
faces that float over the historic
streets of the ancient city, or in the steam
as it rises off the pork cabbage, the chop sticks
painted with the character for happiness —
or in the pitiful words whispering
out of a million needle-eyed mouths.

— Please be kind enough to help us.
— Please change our lives.

And in a series of the strangest
requests, they propose an unusual
cultural exchange of bodies and fates.
And the absurdity — the surprise. They
propose, because it took you too long to say
no, there's no turning back; and because it
took you too long to say no, you've actually
become the noodle-stained waitress as she glides
across the disgusting restaurant
floor, or the wall-eyed man as he bails
leaking buckets of shit from under the streets.
And because it took you too long to say
no, you've become the shy butterfly
girl trying to piece together her father
out of yellowed letters and regrets.

— Won't you please help me, you hear yourself say.
— Please, I need someone.

And what a surprise — the astonishment
when you feel for the first time a million
bovine eyes following the traditional
slit up the side of your rose print flower dress.

— Please, you hear yourself say.

And the absurdity. You're actually
surprised when you feel a million bovine

eyes pass through the slit up the side of your
dress — like it's the gate to the imperial
city — the gate that starts just above your tiny
velvet slippers, goes past the silk black
tops of your stockings — and all the way
home to your little warm bamboo heart.

AROUND MIDNIGHT IN THE EXPRESSIONLESS CITY THREE
EXPATRIATES (AN IMPOSSIBLE COURTIER, A CONSUMMATE
DRUNK, AND A HARMLESS FOOL) CONVERGE FIVE FLIGHTS
UNDER THE SOULFUL SAXOPHONE OF DA HUA

— In my country we would say his immense heart could
fill a room, or a house, or that he's
all heart — a heart with a man inside. I
see this when he plays, on my grandfather's
farm when I was small — the ocean — the cows
standing in knee-deep grass. Some say when he
plays his lips bleed, but I believe
it's his heart, and the beautiful
red drops that fall from his mouth become
music. Drops of blood falling
into dry sand. We can believe this. If we
can believe this, then we can see the music
fall into the street one piece at a time.

— If Hua's up there and I'm on the inside, I want
to shout, "Hey Hua!" Or I want to shout, "It's
me, and I got something, and I got
something, too." Or let's say the years have
piled up into considerable drama, and if I
get started I could flood the whole town solo. Morning
papers read: FOREIGN CRYBABY DROWNS A BILLION
— In tears of Rage and Regret. Instead, I open
the windows, turn down the yellow
electric light, and let the horn blow in
— start feeling right where I am — inside
my head. Hua's got deep bell tones — cotton
refrains asking, "Who? Who is it? Who are you?"

— When Hua plays I imagine his fingers
escaping his hands — or his fingers
falling off line — ten deserting soldiers
finding themselves in the wrong fight — ten fingers
senselessly jubilant, and then without
knowing why, the hands panic and follow — then his
wrists, arms, shoulders. I
imagine this. His mouth saying
"Yes" to years of "You will do this Hua," or "You will
think this Hua." And for years his mouth says
"Yes," but the horn says, "No." I imagine
his horn saying "no" as the music
tumbles into the street. Music
tumbling out of the windows in round
perfect notes — handfuls — up to your
knees. I imagine, as we stand here, the gods
take these notes and make good little children.

MISS ZHOU'S ESSAY CONCERNING SOLITUDE

I want to say how peculiar your
assignment is at me. I want to speak

what-so-ever at how unnatural
it is to be alone like you ask — then

write what I think transparent coming from
my inside. I look over and over, thus

I see nothing until I saw ants
dispatch across the boys' sporting field down

along the garden edge. Moreover, what
they do? I wonder. How happy? Are their

friends with the wind because I think I
felt the wind when I write in face, and saw

flowers and ants dispatch along their own
way. People step on them — Ouch — I never

do that again. Believe please. I'm
telling. I saw for first time before

to live like that and felt sadnesses. Never
could I be such ant or petal

flower. Such as I am, I only felt
strange. When I write thus in my transparent

inside, I felt only things very strange.

EXPATRIATE BABBLE

So many roads. So many lives to lead. Three
expatriates return to their foreign home after
an evening of devilment and madcap
frivolity in the despairing city. One man, still
excited by a romantic possibility, lifts
his hands like he's holding a woman, and then
theatrically mouths seduction as he waltzes
around his empty apartment floor. The second
growls and barks accusingly as the bottom of one
bottle becomes another, feeling
brave in the process, brave in the noise — feeling
for moments that his words are not gibberish, quite
sure that he awes those around him with his
wit and verve. The third man sits
silently and nods, but if he were to speak, the deep
regret in his voice would cloud above him, rain
upon him — until the waters thickened and rose, possibly
drowning him, possibly washing him the ten miles
down the polluted river and into the indistinguishable
yellow foreign sea. And as the black air whirls
around them, they all talk at once, or not talk — defying
the night to continue, defying the stars to move across
the sky, defying the planets to rise. But the night
does continue. The stars and planets do move and rise
— leaving the three exhausted and forlorn by dawn, sitting
in a neat row on the dancer's balcony — full of frowns
— incoherent mockings, or self-contained imaginings of great
ocean waves, the hellish stench of the festering river.

The men sit in such firm solidarity when a truckful
of ducks roars into the bland oriental
street below, exploding the three into unbridled
laughter, exploding their faces into their hands, their
heads between their knees.

"What lives we lead!" shouts the dancer.
"I feel everybody's pain," moans the drunk.

But the third man burns the vision of the truck deep
in his mind, seeing himself as not only behind
the wheel, but inside the cages — sleepily
driving into the end of days, and at the same time
flapping chubby clipped white wings into airless
infinity. And of course, amongst all of it, the ribald
humor. And what of this? He turns to his expatriate
friends, but for nothing. The dancer has returned
to his waltz, and the drunk has returned to his
bark and growl, leaving the reticent man sitting
alone in the great eastern dawn void, wondering
if there was anything funny in the first place
 — or wondering if possibly there's simply
nothing left for any further articulation.

WILLIE LI SPEAKS FROM INSIDE THE SHADOW POEMS

In back of the words — something you almost say:
Camels, Snow White, the moon at home. Or is it

a joke? You're going to laugh anyway — or not
laugh. You're going to do whatever it is

they want you to do. And when they ask what the poems
mean, you say: bray, or moo. And when they

come to get you they'll find no one — or someone
else. They'll escort whoever it is inside

an old black coat into a car, but somewhere
down the road, the coat stops talking. Somewhere

down the road, the coat stops moving — so they'll
use it instead to shine their shoes, wipe

their mouths — they'll stuff it into a crack to block
an unpleasant draft. Or maybe they'll

just toss it out the window because it's gotten
tiresome or dirty — because whatever

it was they wanted, they've forgotten — because
whoever it was you were, you no longer are.

Dream Of Returning To The People's Republic Photographic Studio

Blistering detail. Incredulous possibilities. Tonight the same
horse-faced man with rotten teeth seats you between
a white back-drop and an antediluvian
camera. Or maybe the camera just
winks at your frozen face, and a delighted
photographer scrambles out from under
a shroud. He smokes a cigarette called
"Hope," and re-positions you with his burning
wand. Or maybe, from inside his black
box, someone caught you drifting. Someone saw
you walking deep into your purple
hills. Someone saw you de-barking your
Italian movie star girl friend. And
— the pain. The embarrassment. You apologize:

Please forgive my perfidious self-intrusion.
Please forgive whoever I am.

> Just smile, he says.
> Say: Candy.
> Say: Money.

And sure, sure, this will cost you. This will
cost you plenty. A horse-faced man with
rotten teeth takes your putty
face in his hands. His fingers
smell like shit, and he pushes a little
to the left, then the right — and yes! That's it:

Never before have you looked so perfect.
Never before have you looked so absolutely you.

A camera winks at your freshly plied
face, or maybe a little horse-man with rotten
teeth re-positions you with a cigarette that has
burned down to nothing. Your head follows his
absurd wand — until you laugh. A delighted
photographer scrambles under his
shroud, but before you vaporize into the white
flash, maybe you freeze your face.
Maybe you drift again.

The way the blue ledge touches the lake water.
The way her black hair falls across her smoky brown skin.

                    Just smile, he says.
                    Say: Candy.
                    Say: Money.

NEW YEAR'S EVE IN CHINA—AND DASH IS DEAD

The man known as "Dash" dies and the news
travels halfway around the world — making
Dash's death a global event of sorts
— that's two hyphens together. Don't get
⠀⠀⠀⠀confused or misled; we'd all feel sorry
for Dash, but it's New Year's Eve in China
and Dash is dead — rolled over in his sleep
and left — had something to do, no doubt, or he
had to laugh, laugh, laugh. I hold my furry
face in my hands sitting around thinking
how we'd talk — how he'd talk about the Cleveland
Indians — everything about the Tribe
— a long string of bad years rolled all
⠀⠀⠀⠀together into one big pile of big
all time losers. "A team you could really sink
your life into," said Dash, who always
wanted to be the big man behind
the plate, tamer of wild pitches, bad
tips, tagging out Pete Rose, "…that fucking
son-of-a-bitch," said Dash, whose literary
works deserve to fly over the moon
with him, or out of the park — one of the few
guys around who said something, and at the same
time had something to say besides, "me-me
-me." I hold my furry face in my mitt
thinking about it but can't linger in such
posture since a ninety mile an hour
⠀⠀⠀⠀fast ball could slam in there at any
minute disrupting consciousness and dental

work, and who knows what to do anyway when
it's New Year's Eve in China, and tomorrow
a big balloon will fall out of the sky
in Times Square, and thousands and thousands
of drunk people will be running around
trying to pull each other's clothes off, shouting
"Fuck New Year. We want Dash." Or maybe
          a little encore on the stories please
— Chapter I or II, or something
on guitar, or something to make us laugh, your
most unhappy chronologers of sad
and unfair events. Tonight we write
with our furry faces in our mitts.
Tonight it's New Year's Eve in China
and our good boy Dash is dead.

Fragmentarily Re-Composing Ms. Tan Dan

Her government advocate father beat her black-
eyed and lame — once damaging
her teeth, and let's face it, nothing's
more unattractive. Still, she actually
liked it, explaining with the following
impromptu remarks, "Sure it hurts, but what
doesn't," and "Beats losing an argument."
Couldn't sit for days on that vast unknown
area covered by black stretch
pants. Red shoes. Accusations. Alchemical. Could

create real guilt from mere
consideration. Said I was
disappointing her. Said I was a fine
gentleman in most respects, knowing well that it's
the qualifications that made her so deadly. Hours
later you were carrying your own
cross and nails, and she would be there for you
ready to swing the hammer. A moonwalker in a country

that fox trots. At the Christmas
dance she anti-circumnavigated the university
Communist party and the student
politburo. Called the Dean, "That crazy
March Hare." Brilliantly fitting by the way. Asked
me if I were impersonating Mr. Chips
sitting there forlorn on the edge
of things, trim beard and tweeds.
Had a secret boyfriend in France everyone

knew about — while betrothed
to a German Professor. Her breath could
drop flies. Very American hair. But really
such a fine anti-circumnavigator, and nothing's
more attractive. Just
had to disappear during the demonstrations
 — after admitting to a friend that she often
tired of this bitter life, that she often
wished she were dead — pushing the little
wheels of her bicycle straight faced through
the crowd. Still can feel the gentle
pounding of her hammer — strikingly inward.

Sadie's Last Love Letter To The Imperial Capital

Wind in shatters. Tire tracks on the wet street. All
night rain and trash blow in the headlights, and a man

waves from the corner. All night a man waves
from the corner — like he knows something
 — everything I am to you. He knows me, and he's
seen you take me apart — piece by piece — unbuttoning
loosening and down, and he wants me, too. He
loves me like you did — like you said

you'd never give up on me, and you're giving
up on me because you'll never understand
what I would do for you, and you'll never
understand how much I could give you. Why, I'd

cut off my hands and paint your room. I'd cut
off my hands and spread the blood so you'd
never forget what we did, and I'd cut off my
hands and lie on your bed waiting for you. I'd
stretch out my arms. I'd stretch out the stumps
of my arms and wait to take you in, and there'd be

no way you could leave me. I'd take you in, and you
could never leave me — because I love you.
Darling, this is how much I love you.

The Foreign Photo-Journalist Re-Developing His Tiananmen Love And Death Girl

What I'm telling you is true. Believe it, or
don't believe it, but there was
an encounter, a surrender —
a conception — faces
rising in the developer, the timer
ticking away like a heart, and of course
the darkness. So imagine
putting your film to bed. I mean that's what you
do when you clean up a job — you develop
everything--then throw most of it out. Now
imagine a picture stopping you: the shapes —
composition — you don't know, so you let it
rise and sharpen, and all of a sudden, she's
there. She's turned away slightly — looking
down, but it's the curve of her shoulder. You really
can't see her face, but there's
no mistaking her — so you blow it up, and you
blow it up, and you see she's looking
down at someone — probably
her boyfriend — and with just
the trail of a smile. Such tenderness — the way
her cheek is rounded — you know she must have been
smiling, and the rest of them too, of course. You recognize
their faces. The headbands. Fists in the air. And the line
of her arm extending downward. You imagine
her arm extending toward you. That's what you
really want — since the first time
you saw her — when you just happened

to catch her in the lens, looking
right through you like she could
see inside the camera, or inside
your eyes. Amazing. Finding her in a crowd
of thousands. This is the way it started. Or maybe

it started when you heard
her voice. She spoke English with an American
accent--and French like the women do
back home — tiny bells trembling
in the trees — each note pure and distinct. And now
you can put her back together: picture
and sound. Of course, she would give up
everything. Nothing matters anymore — and you hear
the click and whirl of the camera in your hands. Slogans.
Jargon. Click and whirl.

We are here for the rights of man.
We are here for the unborn generations.

Tiny bells, you think. Flowers. Then you wonder
what it would take. You can feel her face
nestled into your chest, her smooth cool
skin in the morning, and how sweet she would be
under you. You could marry her and live
in your mother's cottage by the sea. You could have
almond-eyed babies, and you remember
looking down and seeing her boyfriend smile.

Everyone smile for PARIS MATCH, you say

and she smiles, click and whirl, and all the lights go
on. Flowers, you think. Her breath smells like
flowers. So amazing. You can actually
smell flowers in the air. Flowers
amongst the garbage and shit of thousands
of people, and out of thousands of flower
girls, you find the queen.

> They think they can kill us, but how
> ridiculous. They think they can kill
> us, but they can't kill the dead.

And her boyfriend nods, but looks away
again when the camera rises, but she
looks right into the lens. She looks right into the lens
like she knows something. And when you look
through the lens at her you think she's the most
provocative woman you've ever seen: the line
of her mouth right before she smiles.

> What do you hope to gain here?

Click and whirl.

> Maybe a life. Just a life.

Tiny bells. Flowers. And when you thank her
you raise your fist in the air, and they
raise their fists in the air, and her boyfriend
says something about freedom before you hear
click and whirl, and now their faces rise

in the developer, and you blow them up, and you blow
them up, and suddenly, it comes
back through the smiles and through the eyes and whatever
happened, happens again: the soldiers
surround the square, and then the soldiers
move in. And you can see everyone running, flushed
into the streets, and there's some shooting. They
think soldiers are shooting
into the air, but there's some shooting
and her boyfriend falls. It's not
a complicated thing. He falls. The soldiers
move on the people, the people
are running, there's some shooting, and her boyfriend
falls. And then her boyfriend dies. And this
should be the end. He's dead. It's enough. But it's
not. The soldiers come and take him, and then the soldiers
come and take her, and it's as if she
never was. She becomes a rumor, confounding
theory, the upsetting story you hear over
a dinner with your Chinese friends
where they tell you, yes, if this is true then
surely this is a bad thing, and you spend
weeks with her picture going from one
official to the next — or one
student to the next.

Do you know her? Is she alive?

And of course no one talks. She doesn't exist
until someone calls you on the phone

and tells you she's been badly wounded — disfigured
in fact. Someone calls you on the phone and tells you
the woman you want is being held
at a factory in the countryside
where she's led naked into a cafeteria and made
to lie across a filthy table on her back.
Or someone calls you and tells you the woman
you want is the most beautiful woman
he's ever seen, and you agree. You agree
looking at her picture — the picture you've
blown up until you can see the men
standing in line, or the men
rocking on top of her telling her to "move
bitch. Move pig." But she doesn't
move. She makes herself numb. She makes herself
poison, and you can almost imagine her
satisfaction as she kills each one. Each one
who touches her dies the slowest, most
agonizing death. Or one day
the phone rings at the hotel and it's her
boyfriend. He wants to tell you your pictures
have incriminated his friends — that because he looked
away — he lives. And he wants to tell you the woman
you're looking for was shot
running down the street. That it was
a simple thing — amazing really. They were running,
there was some shooting, and all of a sudden, she falls;
and then all of a sudden, she dies. But this
is how he'll remember her, he says. Your
pictures in the MATCH. Freedom. The raised
fists. The noiseless shouting, and he stops in mid-

sentence, changes the tone
of his voice, and thanks you. He actually
thanks you, and this should be the end. She's
dead. It's enough. But it's
not. You hang up and look at the picture
you've blown up, the picture
you've blown up until you can see
the trail of a smile on her round cheek, the picture
you've blown up until the cheek and smile
move toward you. She turns her round cheek
towards you, and with her most
provocative smile looks back through the camera — through
the lens like she knows something. Such
tenderness, you think. Bells. Flowers — like birth. She
looks right through you and you feel
your heart beating like a timer, but this time
her smile fades and her beautiful round
cheek flattens. This time she points a finger
straight at your face.

It was you, she says. You.

And it's amazing. You hear her and actually
wonder what it would take to pull the bullets
out of her chest, to pull the factory men
off her legs, to wash the faces out of your
camera. A photographic
impossibility, you think — as she
rises and sharpens in the developer — for
you, or for her boyfriend, for the unborn
generations, or the rights of man. It becomes

unclear picture and sound. But out
of a thousand flower girls, she
lived — and she died. Now, believe it.

Love Letter From The Great Eastern Cold War

Eradicable fate. Storm. Lunar extravaganza.
Every night stupid words fall apart and pile
at my feet, and every night I want to say
something for you. I want to say something
to beam over thousands of miles and materialize
in everything you see. I want to become

the pots when they rattle in the kitchen —
the bark on the dog. I want to become the strange
footprints you find frozen in the snow.
And when you see these things and hear these things

I want you to know I'm there — that I've come
home — just for a minute to say something
to make a difference — to say: hello. So

hello. I've come for just a minute. I've
come for just a minute to stand by you — to see
you — as the words fall apart — as you stand by me.

SOMEWHERE IN THE MIDDLE OF THE AMERICAN POETRY LECTURE, MR. FU ESCAPES INTO THE POSSIBILITIES

It's real world, Mr. Fu. Dream-life. Love, hate, pain
regret, death — trembling through your fingers — through
your lips — the stuff that's left out of every five
year plan. Unimaginable insurrection — even as you
sit at your desk — between the talk and books
and lunch — between a drifting recollective
conversation with your girl friend, or between the moment
you watch a scalding cup of tea slip out of someone's
hand, and the moment it explodes into a million china
stars and planets on the freezing classroom floor. It's not

unimaginable. In a moment a man might close his desk, walk
through the door, past the guard, out of town, down the
road — imagine. Alone on the road— sun baked — feet gone to
black leather, black hands, black face, walking light
and strong. All afternoon, no university sweater and pin. No
five year plan, or all afternoon a man might sleep with his
hat over his face. He might have holes in his pants. He could
have great holes in his pants, and hundreds of miles in all
directions. Now —

sigh. Unilaterally spin
deep into the crazy
purple void. Love, hate, pain, regret
death — all trembling
in front of your eyes. No one
around approving — disapproving
smiles — frowns, pestering

minor officials schooled in
intimidation, bantering
guilt, fashion, centrality. Now —

sigh, in direct proportion to American modern and post-
modern metaphor. Maybe even a shirt made out of
grass — by the plum lake, or by the plum river, with great
worn holes in your pants. All afternoon, or for the rest
of all days and noons, just a man and his
black leather feet — by the mountains, by the sea. Now

momentarily sigh in all directions. It's real
world, Mr. Fu. It's you. So go ahead.

VIEW FROM ROOM 10-02
(At the Hua Dong Hospital)

Ten flights down. I look down and say,
"Ouch," to myself. I look down and see:
piles of coal, laundry on lines, blue
and white ambulances moving slowly around
tiny yellow people. After a blistering

seven day drunk, Roger looks down and sees
his own death walking about the courtyard.

     "There it is," says Rog, pointing to what
he calls, "The Landing Strip," referring
to where we are now as "The Launch Pad," to himself
as "The Bird."
     "The man walking down there is
the dead me," says Roger. "And the dead
me is different from the live me, which is
different from the dead you, which is what
you are," accuses Rog as he bolts towards the locked
balcony door — only to fall on his face, becoming
the comatose him, which nobody feels sorry
about — even though he's cut his head in the spill.

An hour later he wakes shaky and sweet, or shaky
and mean, and wants to put a halo over my
head, tells me, "Thanks," for all I've
done for him, or calls me, "The hollowed-out
ice man."

"You're going to go down cold and alone, you
son-of-a-bitch," says Rog, then asks,
        "Am I going to die?" when his
heart wants to jump out of his chest. I want to say,
"Sure, sometime, but I don't think just yet."

I think of murder as the live me holds his
hand, counting the roaches on the wall while Rog
shakes himself to sleep, but the dead me makes his
way through the locked door to the balcony, where
I look down at a tiny yellow man waving
frantically next to a blue and white
ambulance--yelling something that sounds
an awful lot like, "Mr. Jim — Mr. Jim — Mr. Jim!"

DENYING THE AFTERNOON WITH MISS MEI LI

I want to tell you it was like being inside
a Gauguin: aqua sky, girl with a crescent
smile — honey, triangular face, a flower
dress. There was a bowl of tangerines, burnt
coconut bread, bitter foreign coffee.
The gardener was working — on Sunday, and smiled
in front of his three teeth, and it was warm —
a balcony in December, second floor in the tops
of the palms, but it didn't happen, and I was never
there, and we never walked to the park. She was a short

stick; I was a tall stick; her father was
an engineer, and she never told me
how the government suggested he become a farmer, move
to the Soviet border where the wheat won't
grow with his new wife and one year old. And she
never told me how the government suggested he was
eating too much, and then the government suggested
he was drinking too much water, and after too much
stumbling, sleeping, or smart mouth, the government
suggested he water the wheat with his own blood. Crushed
skull and testicles. Crushed ribs and feet.
It never happened.

I bought her ice cream and she dropped it
in the dirt. And she never came back to sit
on my balcony in the traditional wicker chair — terrific
posture, a little lip stick smudged on her teeth.
Everyone in this country dreams of feeding Deng

Xiaoping to the dogs, she said. Everyone in this
country dreams of the day the blood on his hands
will rise and choke out his life. And she never

leaned back and smiled. Rouge on her cheeks. December
sun. Coconut bread. Bowl of tangerines. Late afternoon
sky going indigo. But what I want to tell you
is this: I'm lying. This never happened. I was never
there. She never lived. Her father never died, and had
I been there, I'd have put my hand over my infected
eyes and ears, shooed her astonishing flower dress
down the stairs, turned up the white noise of the air
conditioner to drown out the neighbors and street
in favor of immediate, progressively
implacable imaginings that Christmas is
coming, that the gardener will fix his teeth, and perhaps
with the purchase of a new hat, I will become Gauguin.

CHECKING IN ON DASH

The mirror of this world. I mean, very
good. All night the moon was holding water over
the Volkswagen building, a lone
star, pulsating purple neon
tirelessly suggesting, "There's
a Volkswagen for you," which
isn't exactly true, is it Dash? I mean it's
not the payments, it's just
the acquisition of those uncompromisable
extras: the wild wide band
radio; the clock that has
no hands; or maybe you got the wants
for wheels that can remember which way's
home. I don't

know. So the next day I'm walking
to the zoo, and every step is good
 — bad-good-bad. I mean that's the way
I see it, block after block with the idea
that I'm looking for something — the subtle
innuendoes of city life, grey dust
rolling down the street, kids screaming
hooray out of school, and today I mean
the wind's got some teeth, a million
troubles, pain, and every step I take
is love — hate-love-hate, and that's very

good, the way I see it: the crescent
moon; the Volkswagen building; lone

star; and me shelling peanuts
all over the concrete. And the kids
say, "Hey, hello Mr. Big Nose Hairy Red
Monster," and I say, "Why, hello
little mice," and they laugh
— cry-laugh-cry, and I laugh
— cry, hold my belly or hold
my head — or not. I'm saying

I'm on my way to the zoo, and the animals
are waiting for me — happy-sad
— or something, and it's been days since I
last had the idea of something
to eat. Who knows? Good Lord
my goodness, Dash. I'm saying I'm
not talking. Very Good. Subtle
innuendoes, tuned to that extra
wild band reception, a little
tick, tick, tick, and wheels
rolling you all the way home.

Is that what it's like being dead?

A Foreign Tale Of Exemplum And Woe

World-wide celebration. Cool strain of wind. Under
yellow lights two expatriates follow contagious
palm lined streets towards the invitation of a roomful
of Chinese girls. One man opens and closes his mouth
excitedly as he walks.
                    "Tonight, my friend, let's
rub the fuzz on a Szechuan peach. Let's float
backwards up the Yangtze."
                              He laughs and tilts back his
head, imagining his words spiraling upwards past
balconies full of damp laundry and caged
condemned chickens. He imagines his words
cloudborne, windborne, making their way
upward until they rest at the feet of some
fiery eyed brown skinned god. Then he imagines
godly trembling, godly steam, clear and distinct
godly facial expressions of disgust and negation.
With this in mind the expatriate lowers his head
and turns to his friend.
                    "It is better to be a prisoner
in my country than a free man here."
                              He pauses
in thoughtful posture, and as he speaks to his
friend and the street lights and the wandering red
planets, the past envelopes him.
                              "Once," he says, and "I
remember," and "Then there was better
beer, music, and women."
                    The friend listens to these
stories of the past with personal

trepidation. For him, the past was full of women who
stole from him. His music was played
out of tune, and the beer he drank made him crazy. He confesses
all of this. He confesses, for him, it is
the future — anxious possibilities. A woman might
love him. She might be tender — compassionate. She
could be for him, and he could be for her. And they
could duplicate themselves with children. They would be
inseparable. And as he speaks his hands fall to his
sides so his children can take hold.

                                        "My
wife," he says. "My children."

                                                He tilts his head
backwards and imagines his words rising upward past
the steep, treacherous sides of a mountain to finally
rest at the feet of some benevolent reclining
god. And there will be fine music. And there will be
the right beer.

                              "My brother, there is nothing more."
And his expatriate brother agrees —
laughing, his head back, already
smelling the amber perfume of a woman he knew
years ago.

They stand frozen in such ecstasy
when a bus roars out of the darkness and flattens
both, the man of the past and the man of the future, into
two bloody heaps of foreign cotton. The next day thrifty
neighbor women collect the blood soaked rags and weave
a rug wide and beautiful that is placed in the foyer
of a collective grocery where people often
congregate to chat about the day's events, and it is
said, when the news arrived in heaven of the expatriates'
death, the gods proclaimed all was right
and well, and that the two men were bound to end in tatters.

The Inscrutable Miss Mei Li Foretells The Future

What you will come to realize is that it's
a big country — doors open, doors close, and whatever
you think is true will turn out to be the thinnest
oil on water, spectacular veil, grey shadow. Your pretty
smooth-faced student, for example. It will
upset you when you learn she sells herself for
food — winter clothes, and the day you meet
her on the street bundled in white fur and red
wool, you will wonder how many times she had to
climb the Spanish professor, how many times
she had to smell his drunken breath as he
fell asleep. And a few weeks later over Latin
coffee and an impassioned discussion of a literary
magazine, he will turn an aside, and with his most
theatrical frown tell you, she had no cherry. Gone
— he will say, flipping his soft, pink
fingers into the air — a very practiced
gesture, you will think, but very
effective. You even imagine a grand release

of doves, or you will imagine how
stupid you must have sounded in the classroom
— the continual pronouncements. Do what you
want with your life. You told this to students
while you watched them shiver in their
concrete box, cold chapped hands around
their pencils, or cold chapped hands
around their throats. You will come to realize
it's the same — that your rather pleasant
apartment on the fourth floor is the same
as the secret black rooms you'll

discover in the basement — except, of course
your leash is longer, your insomnia is self-
induced, the circles you pace are wider, and the tiny
screams you hear are in another language. And you

will come to realize the government did not
lie. No one was killed at Tiananmen Square, or the mass
graves that hold the thousands who did die are
small holes in a country of mass graves. Doors
open, and doors close. It's a big country. Or maybe
it's really a study in syllogistic
insignificance — starting with the premise: You are
nothing. Your life is worth nothing, so when we
kill you, we really can't kill you. You're

already dead. And you will feel dead when you
glide down the streets in your European
sport coat — the yellow-milk people spilling
around you, the neon pulsating
sadness of endless charcoal evenings. And months
from now when you return to your own country, during
the most important football game of the year, the men
will ask you, does Chinese pussy taste the same, or if
you've been to the pre-eminent oriental bar over
a hundred yards long — as the renown full-back
stumbles into the end zone, as the defense
systematically destroys the boy-god quarterback
— you'll feel dead — a clumsy wandering
spirit. You will come to realize. In a big
country, doors open and doors close — perhaps
even as your hands grip the wheel during the long
white drive north from the metropolitan airport, into
whatever it is you're going to try to call your life.

II

"It is not down in any map; true places never are."

Ishamael, *Moby Dick*

How To Arrive In Faraway Places

Mechanically fall through an impulsive
bruised sky full of capillary lightning.

Sit pressed to a gargantuan flowered
suitcase and a praying Mozambiquian
woman who says: If Madre Deus
wills, we will die together.

Live and applaud. Be sure to applaud
with everyone else when the plane
bounces to a landing —
                          the grinding
of hot metal raising a collaborative
groan throughout the economy cabin
 — the spilling of passengers
into the anesthetized deep water
darkness —
                to the toll of church bells
 — into rain so thick, you could
make your own bone soup.
                          Spill into a crowd
that stares as if you're some magnificent
green bird, as if you'll metamorphose
into someone they'll know
                          — loving, kind
husband; blessed Father; crazy uncle; kid
brother; mythic fool — whatever
you want, whoever you become: Take

your chances. Square up your mighty
football shoulders, swing those
bags, and smile, smile, smile.

FOR THE T'AI CHI MASTER, GEORGE YOUNG (IN THE CELEBRATED AND ENCUMBERED STUDENT/ MASTER TRADITION)

I am running down the beach with the full
wind in my face, and I am running just the way
you taught us — the sound of your voice
calling me in. With the sound of your voice
calling me in, I am your swallow — flying
home to roost. I am floating, beautifully
aligned — just the way you taught us with my feet
scarcely above the hard packed sand, or maybe I am

running just above the long white plume of my own
breath, my arms slicing through the air. I am
pushing my arms through my breath, above
my breath, as my breath moves along the sand, I
close my eyes — just the way
you taught us. I close my eyes, and when I

open them, I have strayed out over the water, far
out in the sea along the red road the sun makes
when it first rises. The red road. I am
traveling the red road, and when I
open my eyes and see the sun, I throw my
arms in the air and shout: Behold — just the way
you taught us in the great spiritual tradition, I

open my eyes and shout: Behold —
as my breath moves over the water, as my breath
flows in and out in jubilation, I become
your tiger running far across the sea. In the true
and ancient tiger tradition — I am

running for you inside my own plume white breath
east across the ocean in Behold jubilation — along
the red road that could go — on a day such as this
 — clear across the fierce and white-capped
Atlantic, and all the way to Portugal.

Every Day Somewhere Along The Big Road

So strange. Amongst a thousand faces. In the bright
sun. A herd of cows passes through the foreign quadra-
toned town that invented good, kind drunken
men, round smiling women who believe
in bleach — in miracles.
                              You have come so
far, and now for even a miracle of your

own: you see the people see you, or you
listen to them call you someone else's
name, and it's OK — definitive — their belief
that something overlaps, or their hope
that someone's similarities will pass
over your face and become
reusable. You're not

unlike someone they know. Can you imagine?
— and of course you can — the mix-up
— the merge — your clothes, for example —
even the color of your words, or the small
beads of perspiration that appear on your face
out of nowhere, perhaps in order to define

how many years it will take to arrive
or return to wherever it is you're going
— as if you really do
belong somewhere, as if
some day you'll appear in your own
town and everyone will open their

doors and shout, "Wow!" How many

years? Perhaps after a series of long
afternoons, or after a series of evenings
when the wind might change over dinner
 — or it becomes cool — possibly bringing
along a little rain. How many years?
You don't know. It's all so strange, and you have

come far into strange talk, into a strange
bleached quadra-toned town filled with smiling
cows, bright shining men and women — all printed
deep into the lines of your face, all an ungodly
wash of incorruptible revelation
 — where you miraculously realize
 — as a chorus of neighbor dogs comes
galloping to greet you, as you brush
foreign confetti from your hair —
whoever it is you are, once again, you've arrived.

POSTCARD FROM THE COBBLE-STONE CITY

A thousand miles from home the road rises — or six
miles from town there's a cliff by the sea, or if
you walk into the hills little clouds of dust
follow your feet for hours. It's just like that

George. Take today, for example. Wake up before
dawn. Get the chills in the asymmetrical
town with the blue/black sky — where every cow plays
its own symphonic bell. The ancient horse is tethered
dangerously by his leg. And other details. I wake

up before dawn and pretend you're alive — listening
to the details — round face in an over-stuffed chair —
cancerous hands, old legs, old heart. I wake up before
dawn and pretend you can read every word
I write. I pretend it means something to you, that you'll
comment to your friends at lunch, or to the post
man, or to your wife. I even pretend you'll be pleased to know

I am well — ardently optimistic — today, for example. Do you
know what I'm doing? I'm taking you in my arms. That's
right. Today, I'm taking you in my arms and flying
you against the spin of this world until you materialize
in everything I see. And I will brush the dust
out of your face, and I will put tools back in your
hands — because it's just like that — as the road rises past
green tea and corn, in the happy-sad village, on the remote
volcanic island, in the middle of the purple, rock
salt sea. Today, you will be pleased to know, I am
pretending — even now, and of course, other details.

Hello George.

Inheriting The Crazy Man's Desk

After all, you put him together as if
he were made of so many pieces of shattered
glass. The landlady's speculation on his
jump into the sea, for instance.

> "By the Mother of God he disappeared
> himself," she tells you. "And now
> lives in perfect heaven we hopes."

She crosses her chest and looks upward — knocks
on the desk top — explaining never was there
a man so kind to wagging-tailed dogs. Never
was there a man so gracious with naughty children.

And of course, let's not forget his face. You can
almost see its thin angles in the perfect
varnish finish: the deep set eyes, the years of bitter
disappoint it takes to create such
a compassionate smile. And you image
his fingers following the gentle swirl in the junglewood
grain, the way he'd sit erect and brave when his pen
said the right things — the way he'd slouch
when the world went wrong. And as you look
out the windows to the sea, or into the tops
of the palms, you can

see him — his vacuum loneliness — listen to the rapt
compelling conversations he had
with himself and whatever it was outside — babies

crying in the neighbor's apartment, street
dogs in a fight — as one evening becomes
the next in the rustling of the trees. You even

imagine him knocking at the door, asking
for his life back, wanting to sit for just
a moment behind the rattling black typewriter — open
a few drawers, lean back into the plush
comfortable chair on wheels.

       "For sustenance," he might say — smiling.
       "By rights, or by the grace of God."

And with his great open smile, he suggests
you follow him through the narrow, winding
island city — because there are so many
lives to lead, because the walking's always
ecstasy under a soft, round
butter moon — because he's found a crack in this
noisy world, and if you're willing
he'll gladly show you how to tumble in.

ON THE BUS

Grandmother prays for the baby on her lap —
or for her haloed brother the ticket man, or she

prays in general on a rosary
worn and beautiful like the one
swinging from the rear-view mirror for the sacred
heart of Jesus, may we all be
safe and delivered from harm on this

funereal roller-coaster — or we can
pray to the bouncing cross on the driver's
tan bare chest — just above the tattoo
that says, Death is my Mistress, which no one
can deny. A man with such a big soul and easy
laugh, I will pray for you, because we're all

flesh and bones. And because we're all
flesh and bones, I think it is better

to hurry so we can watch
the bracelets swing on the delicate
wrists of the young girl in the beautiful
Italian dress, or watch the scarf
sway in her hair, or we can
see the end of this pathetic island road
disappear into the profound
blue sea. So close. So deep. Hurry

please, I want to tell the driver. The young
man standing in the back with the smooth
face and slicked-back hair is in love, and today
we have hopes. Today, we are all completely
filled with these great exasperating hopes.

THE AVAILABLE SUPPORTING FEMALE ROLES
(From the Modern Latin Theatre)

She can play somebody's little girl — wearing
a purple slap on her cheek. She's
fifteen — holding hands with her boyfriend
 — in the night doorway, inside the city
famous for listening to its own
breathing. It's a dark street under
a bowlful of stars. Or when the street

fills with stars, she can play her own
heartache — the trembling round-shouldered
woman at the bus stop in the Italian
design, fine contemporary hair — or she's
round-bellied and waddling. She's
your mother, your daughter — your
wife. She's twenty, or inside
the faint blue rim of the TV, she becomes
thirty-five — her life etched into her face.

The church clock ticks in the church tower.
Blue and white fishing boats roll in the fishing
boat harbor, and with each sea-swell

she opens and closes her eyes; and with each
sea swell, the world falls deeper into a looking
glass. "Who is it?" she says, or "Say 'Hello'
to what you've become." And this time she
becomes the skull in the second
story window, or the little

fist that knocks on her own
door saying, "Anybody in there?"

As the street fills up with stars.
As the city breathes in and out, she plays

the talking hole in her own face. "No.
No," it says. "Nobody. I don't think so. No."

CIRCLING THE HOUSE AND GROUNDS
OF HENRIQUE BERNARDO

Even the dust behaved for him. It would lie
still on the edge of the vineyard until he
told it to do this or that. And the grapes
behaved too, following the lines he had
strung about a foot off the ground— because
of the wind, he said. He pointed to the sky
and said, "the wind," but later when he
pointed to the sky we didn't catch whether
it was the wind or God who had taken
his wife. It doesn't matter, of course. The grapes

grew anyway, and he made wine just like
his father had taught him, even putting it
in the same bottles—which amazed us—as did
the tour of his spotless house. Imagine
following him through the dark hallways
as he pronounces the name of each
room in a strong, clear voice: kitchen
bathroom, bedroom—his clothes
already carefully laid out for church—
until he stops in front of a picture
of his wife, kisses the glass
in front of her face—and bursts into tears.

He was a big man, and there was no
telling how much wine it would take him
to get to the end of the afternoon.

ANOTHER TUNE PLAYED BLUE
(For Mother On My 38ᵗʰ Birthday)

The falling debris of countless days. It's the way
it happens. I wake up in the middle of the night
dreaming we're in a war movie. I wake up, rub my
sleepy head so hard we're in France, or London —
it doesn't matter where — and we're talking — which
seems very fitting. We are talking, and as we
talk the planes get closer and closer, and we talk
and talk, and the planes get closer and closer, until
people in the audience — out of an unabashed
desire to resolve tension start shouting, "Air
Raid! Air Raid!" But we can't hear them, of course —
we just go right on talking while everyone watches
whistling bombs drop out of the planes. Everyone
covers their eyes with their hands, peeks through
their fingers, watching us go on and on — two slowly
deflating balloons, I think — until somewhere
in the middle of some ridiculous gesture everything
goes — Wham — and I'm concrete and you're abstract.

So I wake up in the middle of the night in some
marginal, unpleasant, remote place — rub my sleepy
crucial head hard enough to see moons, sun, stars —
thinking: maybe it was a war movie. Maybe the lights
will go on and an audience will slowly file
out and congregate under a marquee — talk about
our effective acting — make plans for a late dinner
— almost in a whisper. But, of course, there's no

dream. No movie. Instead, after four days of hard
rain, I wake up in the middle of the night
and listen to wind come off the ocean. I listen
to the wind come off the ocean — thinking
of words I might say to you if you were
to return — words that could define you, or us —
words that could coerce you to stay for just
a moment, to take a breath, a cup
of tea, or even a small piece
of conversation that could last us both
until our days run back together. So I

listen, as the wind comes off the water
bringing on a little rain — thinking: where
are you? Thinking: can you hear me? Thinking:
sometimes in the middle of the night, I think
I can hear the distant hum of approaching planes.

In Dreams Eduarda Maria Is In Love And Living In Paris

The afternoon light is soft, and it
drops into my courtyard the way
flowers drop from the trees — a petal
at a time, I think — and I think
the courtyard is completely
filled with flowers, and my room as well
 — a box of flowered light, or a box

of sun, and this light and sun
float down and sink into everyone's
face and eyes — deep into the evening
and the evening streets. I walk
the smoky evening streets and watch
the dim shine in everyone's
face, or listen to their soft

murmuring voices as they
hold each other in their flower
petal rooms — their arms and legs
and the light in their faces
holding them together, all
together breathing the same air. I
listen and see this from deep

in someone's arms — watch the dim
shine come off his face — from the hollow
of his wide shoulder — and listen
to his promises — all night.
All night the light comes off
his face and he holds me. All
night he promises to never let me go.

A Cerebral Return To The Days Of Descending The Great Hill At Faja Da Cima

So now the days compress themselves. You
become the moment that happened between
the horse eating his grain and the old
woman sweeping the doorway — or the old

man with the three-foot stick of bread will
remember you to the café owner's beautiful
daughter. "Maria, he was the thing that blew
by us like something out from the sea." And her

laugh will float out into the street
and rise to the rooftops. Her laugh will rise
out and circle around them — and you will
become the thing that draws them together. For
years to come you will draw them together
 — and for this they will make you
real again: the strange cut of your
clothes — the odd foreign man riding
his bike — damp eyes, damp hair — and when they

make you real she will
laugh, and when she laughs the years will
flood out of his pale bent body and he'll
want to take her in his arms. He'll want to
take her in his arms and slowly
roll all night inside the sound your wheels made
somewhere along a long stretch of downhill road.

The House Called Nossa Senhora Da Boa Viagem

The old woman shook the sheets once a week
under the blue and white plaque of the doorway
and chased dust with a rag mop and a bottle
of bleach.

       And once a week the gardener would study
the banana plantation like there was something
more to understand, maybe prophecy or inspiration
written on the broad leaves or the rotting
fruit at his feet.

When it rained the house stood against the rain
 — her roof shooting water well off the walls.
In the sun, she opened her eyes, every window
a lantern forever calling someone home.

Once, when we asked, the old lady said the Dono
went west and pointed at the shadowy hole
in the ocean left by the sun after it set.
"And maybe he will return — this evening
or the next. You see, a good man will come home
and a good house must be ready to welcome him."

We lived in that town all winter and spring until
the red volcanic roads turned into swirling
dust, until we saw the gardener, house, and old
lady disappear under the silver wing of a dream-
bound plane.

Nossa Senhora Da Boa Viagem: Our
Lady of Good Travels, of Good Voyage, may we
travel well. Keep our hearts in your hands. Keep us
dry and warm and full of your light. Keep us
all until we get to wherever we're going.

The Miraculous Academic Departure Of Little Ana Of God

I am sitting on a beach two thousand miles
away from you with my hands in the air — facing
your general direction. The ocean's gray-
green and full of words, and the neighboring
town and dunes are full of powerful, artistic
influential people out to salt the earth — which isn't
unlike the man who failed you, I guess. He deserves
to be flogged with his own dangling modifier and stretched
for revision on a spit, which is really kind of
pathetic, isn't it, or so unimaginably
real it could be horrifically framed in the wings
of lost angels and hung in the New York Metropolitan
Museum of Art — like your hands, for instance. I mean

they're not even like hands — flippers is more
like it. And when you take a pencil in your flipper
it disappears inside strange folds, frustrations
sadness — strange Portuguese sadness — and pain past
remedy. And then there are your legs. They're
more or less stumps, pushing against the ground while
everyone glides around you. Everyone
is gliding around you and you're getting
nowhere. You ask God, Jesus, and of course
Fatima — the great and wholly compassionate patron
saint of Portugal for help, and in your dreams

they help you. In your dreams they turn you into
a sea gull. They make you beautiful in your dreams
— and light, so profoundly beautiful and light, you rise

out of your bed, through the roof, pass over
the humiliating university, higher and higher, until
the world is a tiny blue-green speck
in blackness. You fly so far away the world
is only another roving ball of light, and there's
nothing you don't know, and there's nothing you can't do.

And this is how you wake in the morning. You wake
so full of knowing that you don't stumble through
the uneven, cubistic streets to the perpetually
incarcerating university. Instead, you go
to the beach and watch gulls circle and bend
in the wind. You go to the beach and look out
at the cresting unforgiving waves, put your
cartoon face into the full wind, spread out your secret
wings in separate, complete aloneness
— in the clandestine full compositional
pain of all the great liberators and saints — and fly.

And this is how I see you from two thousand
miles away, from another beach, at the other end
of the ocean. The water's gray-green
and conversational. The weather's terrible and thick
with gulls who can do anything in the full wind — like
you, I guess — so much like you I am sitting here with my
big ears listening, asking God, Jesus, and of course the great
and compassionate Fatima to let you know — I
know who you are. I am sitting on this beach with my
hands in the air — waving my best hello and good-bye
to the gulls — watching for the one
who's waving hello and good-bye back in Portuguese.

The Return Of The Inscrutable Miss Mei Li

I write to you so excited Jim Brother thinking
you read this and remember how time flies. Thinking
you read this I ask now — How are you? What you
do? Now long ago I look in Shanghai for you return but no
see. Many people ask me — Where and who is Jim? And I
say: No. I don't know — which is very sadnesses since I
think you many times. I wait month and lose
hopes — look up in dark sky. My Brother. In winter I meet

a Germany man. We love each other since second time we
meet. He travel in China and like China very well in spring
we propose marriage and ceremony at famous Hong Zhou
factory where many my friends in celebration
and happy — but I never forget and wish you Jim
Brother was there and happy too. I think many times I see
you big face in music and people dance full of great
happinesses until I remember no, you no there and I
cry in my inside. In September we come to Germany

land where his parents live and it is very beautiful but we
find no flat and live his parents good people but no
speak English so I learn Germany very hard and help his
mother whenever I can. In six months think I speak
Germany very well and now tell you how excited since maybe
we get baby. I like Childrens very well, but miss China
and friend, and I think and wonder are you married
and happinessed, too? For long time ago you asked: Do I
forget you — and I say: No! — and tell you helped me in many
things I never forget and tell you time flies but I never

forget and wish I could hear words from you and finally
wish you in my deepness heart, my Brother, somewhere
you read this and send
happinessed words back to me, and tell me since last
time we meet, you have big smile and many, many wells.

BELATED LETTER OF THANKS
TO DA WANG AND DAUGHTER

What can we say for ourselves after so much
time? What's the measure? Another day of roar becomes
evening, and I can still see you — a nice man — a man
given to peaceful loving routines. Or I can
say, we were all peaceful in a time
not known for its peace — for example, a month after
the Red Army bulldozed a human landfill around
Beijing, I bought greasy pecan cookies three
evenings a week at the market, and you

rode by on your bicycle in the darkness.
You were the man with the big smile, singing
to his tiny little girl — a girl so small, I
even thought, in the darkness, if she might be
a bag of oranges. But she was no
bag of oranges, and you were no soldier, only
a lullaby bike rider, and I was just
a cookie man. For years now when the evening comes

down, we've stayed like this: me, a bumbling big
faced foreign man strolling mindlessly under
a parasol of trees with Chinese cookie grease
bleeding through a brown bag--and you
pedaling through the darkness with your most
precious cargo. I just

wanted to say: "Hello, Mr. Wang." I just
wanted to wish you well, and thank you for
singing songs that have kept the darkness
friendly — all these years — little songs
wrapped in a circle of dust, stretching
from one side of night to the other.

WE GYPSIES

Fortune moves us — the canary yellow
wagon, the blue roan horse, our wheels
finding every pothole in the kingdom. I'm

a smiler (the conjurer's deception)
taking money from games of shells. You sing,
sell luck or considerable
longing from your dance, and under round
stars, when the good people come
for their small coins, we ask

the pots not to bang, wrap the horse's
shoes in rags, and steal the road.
And always, floating
through black air, your head's
on my lap. Sometimes you make it clear

this life stinks. You want your own
whitewash, thatch, and cow, and ask
over a bucket of tears, what I'm
going to do about it. So I drop

the lines, let the horse
have his head, and slowly make
my way through your scarves
and into the folds of your wild
dress, until unmistakably
you know we've made it home.

In The Middle Of The Tall Night In The Cobble-Stone City, Captain James — The Sailor Man — Heads For Home

All the love wrapped around itself
inside the windows above the dark

street. I hear everybody's small
painful voice — in the painful
wash of days and days. Blue night —
the way I feel on this blue night
and not one sound. I walk
down to the fishing boat harbor
my arms wide. I'm saying

I'm walking down to the foreign harbor
with the whole city inside my head
and ten waves taller than a house
roll in. Ten waves saying: I'm
going to kill you, James. Or ten
waves saying: Just you wait. So I
wait. I know. I wait. It's a blue

night, and a little wind ruffles
the curtains above the street, and I
say: So quiet for you. This deep
peace--and I listen to the foreign
sad breathing in and out. I

listen. Maybe, my wife, I
think. Maybe my little boy. I listen
until I have to go, and then

I go — the way I feel — a big
fat moon all wrapped
around itself — and me
whispering up to the fluttering
windows: Sleep tight. Sleep tight.

The Expatriate Returns To Dream Street

A thousand days pass, and then a thousand
more. The person you were returns
home to the pretty hill town where smoke
rises straight out of the chimneys, flowers
bloom, or you skate through
ice and snow. It doesn't matter. This
is your town, and you're home.
A thousand days pass, and then a thousand

more. The streets you know curve and wind, but it's
dark, or almost light. It doesn't
matter. You know the way — warm or cold — every
square or round window, every
dog and cat, as if nothing changes
 — nothing goes away. A thousand days

pass. Your house is almost the same. Boards
sag. Colors fade in the kitchen light. Inside
you see — your beautiful wife; your angelic
daughter; the reasonable, prideful
version of yourself. And as if you have
something to say, you press your oily
face into the window glass; you press your
face just as close as you can get, or you press

your ear to the door and listen to their paper
voices laugh — your long brittle fingers
tapping a rhythm into the wood. You
hope they might hear. You hope they actually
hear you say: Hello. Hello
in there. It's me. Let me in. And I'm home.

Fomite

A fomite is a medium capable of transmitting infectious organisms from one individual to another.

"The activity of art is based on the capacity of people to be infected by the feelings of others." Tolstoy, *What Is Art?*

Writing a review on Amazon, Good Reads, Shelfari, Library Thing or other social media sites for readers will help the progress of independent publishing. To submit a review, go to the book page on any of the sites and follow the links for reviews. Books from independent presses rely on reader to reader communications.

For more information or to order any of our books, visit
http://www.fomitepress.com/FOMITE/Our_Books.html

The Way None
of This Happened
Mike Breiner

The Moment Before an Injury
Joshua Amses

Nothing Beside Remains
Jaysinh Birjépatil

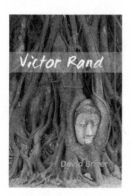

Cycling in Plato's Cave
David Cavanagh

Victor Rand
David Brizer

Picking Up the Bodies
James F. Connolly

Fomite

Unfinished Stories of Girls
Catherine Zobal Dent

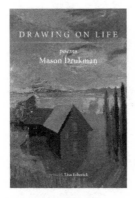

Drawing on Life
Mason Drukman

*Foreign Tales of
Exemplum and Woe*
J. C. Ellefson

Free Fall/Caída libre
Tina Escaja

Sinfonia Bulgarica
Zdravka Evtimova

Derail Thie Train Wreck
Daniel Forbes

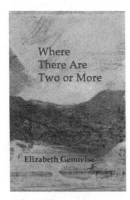

*Where There Are Two or
More*
Elizabeth Genovise

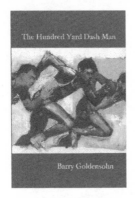

*The Hundred Yard
Dash Man*
Barry Goldensohn

*When You Remeber
Deir Yassin*
R. L. Green

Fomite

*A Guide
to the Western Slopes*
Roger Lebovitz

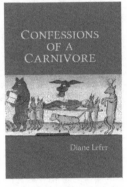

Confessions of a Carnivore
Diane Lefer

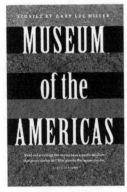

Museum of the Americas
Gary Lee Miller

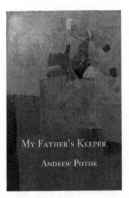

My Father's Keeper
Andrew Potok

*The Hole That Runs
Through Utopia*
Joseph D. Reich

Companion Plants
Kathryn Roberts

Rafi's World
Fred Russell

*My Murder
and Other Local News*
David Schein

Bread & Sentences
Peter Schumann

Fomite

Principles of Navigation
Lynn Sloan

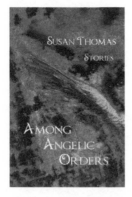

Among Angelic Orders
Susan Thoma

Everyone Lives Here
Sharon Webster

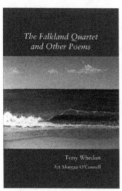

The Falkland Quartet
Tony Whedon

*The Return of
Jason Green*
Suzi Wizowaty

*The Inconveniece
of the Wings*
Silas Dent Zobal

Fomite

More Titles from Fomite...

Joshua Amses — *Raven or Crow*

Joshua Amses — *The Moment Before an Injury*

Jaysinh Birjepatil — *The Good Muslim of Jackson Heights*

Antonello Borra — *Alfabestiario*

Antonello Borra — *AlphaBetaBestiario*

Jay Boyer — *Flight*

Dan Chodorkoff — *Loisada*

Michael Cocchiarale — *Still Time*

Greg Delanty — *Loosestrife*

Zdravka Evtimova — *Carts and Other Stories*

Anna Faktorovich — *Improvisational Arguments*

Derek Furr — *Suite for Three Voices*

Stephen Goldberg — *Screwed*

Barry Goldensohn — *The Listener Aspires to the Condition of Music*

Greg Guma — *Dons of Time*

Andrei Guruianu — *Body of Work*

Ron Jacobs — *The Co-Conspirator's Tale*

Ron Jacobs — *Short Order Frame Up*

Ron Jacobs — *All the Sinners Saints*

Kate MaGill — *Roadworthy Creature, Roadworthy Craft*

Ilan Mochari — *Zinsky the Obscure*

Jennifer Moses — *Visiting Hours*

Sherry Olson — *Four-Way Stop*

Janice Miller Potter — *Meanwell*

Jack Pulaski — *Love's Labours*

Charles Rafferty — *Saturday Night at Magellan's*

Fomite